THE

OF

HOPE

ADVENT AND CHRISTMAS
REFLECTIONS
IN THE
HOLY CROSS TRADITION

Edited by
ANDREW GAWRYCH, C.S.C.

ave maria press AmP notre dame, indiana

© 2009 by Priests of Holy Cross, Indiana Province

Founded in 1865, Ave Maria Press is a ministry of the Indiana Province of Holy Cross.

www.avemariapress.com

ISBN-10 1-59471-221-2   ISBN-13 978-1-59471-221-0

Cover image © jiunlimited.com.

Cover and text design by John R. Carson.

Printed and bound in the United States of America.

INTRODUCTION

✠

THE GIFT OF hope is in many ways the gift of the Advent and Christmas seasons. In Advent we begin our new year as God's people. We seek to rekindle our hope by remembering what God has done for us in the past, by becoming evermore aware of what he continues to do for us in the present, and by turning our gaze toward what he has pledged to do for us in the future.

There is nothing more powerful that God does for us than coming and making his dwelling among us. In fact, the word *advent* comes from the Latin word *adventus* meaning *coming*. So in Advent, we recall in a particular way how God came to be a part of our human family in past generations, how God continues to come into our lives in the here and now, and how God has promised to come and be the consummation of our world at the end of time.

All of this recollecting and reflecting in Advent, of course, prepares us for the celebration of Christmas. During the Christmas season we rejoice and give thanks with awe and wonder for the coming of God in the Incarnation. We learn in the Incarnation that God so loved the world and so longed to be with us that he sent his only Son to become one of us. Conceived through the power of the Holy Spirit and born of the Virgin Mary in a stable in Bethlehem, Jesus of Nazareth was the definitive coming of God to dwell among us. It is this coming, this advent of our Lord to dwell among us, that brings us the true gift of hope—the hope of Emmanuel, God-with-us.

We, the priests, brothers, and sisters of Holy Cross, are men and women with hope to bring. Named after Sainte Croix, the small town in France where we were founded by Blessed Basil Moreau in 1837, we seek to bring the gift of hope to our schools, universities, parishes, and other ministries spread over five continents. We do this by coming and dwelling among the people with whom God plants us in each particular place. We strive to be not just their servants, but their neighbors—to be truly with and of God's people. For, like them, we are burdened by the same struggles and beset by the same weaknesses; like them, we are made new by the same Lord's love; like them, we hope for a world where justice and love prevail.

Through the reflections of this book, we invite others to dwell with us during the seasons of Advent and Christmas so that we might share the transforming hope we have found through our lives and ministry in Holy Cross. Along the way, the major themes of our Holy Cross tradition emerge in the reflections. They include our trust in Divine Providence, our familial spirit and unity, our eucharistic fellowship and worship, our belief that education is both of the mind and the heart, our apostolic zeal to make God known, loved, and served, and our trust that even the Cross can be borne as a gift.

The reflections, written by Holy Cross priests, brothers, and sisters from around the world, begin on the First Sunday of

Advent and continue through the twelve days of Christmas to the traditional celebration of Epiphany on January 6. Each reflection begins with a passage from the scripture readings for the day. The Sunday readings come from Cycle A. The reflections are meant to be read—ideally alongside the daily scripture readings—as part of personal, familial, or communal prayer and meditation each day.

We pray that these daily reflections will enliven your journey through Advent and Christmas so that having become ever more aware of how God dwells in our midst, you will discover anew the gift of hope. For God, indeed, is with us.

Andrew Gawrych, C.S.C.

A Note on the Calendar

✠

The number of days in Advent varies depending upon which day of the week Christmas falls. This booklet contains entries for all the possible days of Advent. They would all be used when Christmas falls on a Sunday. In other years, there will be "extra" entries in the booklet.

- On December 17 of any year, please turn to the entry for that day and follow the calendar dates from there on.
- The entry for the celebration of the feast of the Holy Family has been placed right after Christmas. Please turn to this entry on the Sunday after Christmas rather than to the entry appointed for that date.

- The traditional date for the Epiphany is January 6, the twelfth day of Christmas. This booklet places it on that date. However, in the United States this feast is observed on the Sunday after January 1. You may prefer to use the Epiphany entry on that Sunday.

First Sunday

You know what time it is, how it is now the moment for you to wake from sleep. For salvation is nearer to us now than when we became believers; the night is far gone, the day is near.

—Romans 13:11–12

ON THIS FIRST Sunday of Advent, we begin . . . at the end. We begin a new church year by celebrating the Last Things, the Second Coming, the end times. There is no mention today of the baby in the manger, no angelic proclamation to Mary, no "Silent Night." No, today the church invites us to begin to calm our hearts and our lives so that we can together focus on one thing: hope.

What do we hope for? The coming of Christ. Later in Advent we will shift our attention to the time before Jesus' first coming—the Incarnation. At this moment, however, we think about how it will all end. This in itself sounds rather ominous. Who wants to think about death or the final judgment or heaven or hell? Well . . . *we* do! St. Paul today urges us to keep these realities close, especially during Advent. For the Christian, the end of this world does not frighten us or fill us with dread; instead, it fills us with unparalleled hope because we know how the story of this world, ultimately written by the God who sent his Son as one of us, will end. As we pray at every Mass, "we wait in joyful hope" for these things to happen. We may still be anxious as to *how* we will die, but we should never ever fear what will happen *when* we die.

And the reality is that our salvation is nearer now than when we first began! In truth, we can make this proclamation every day of our lives. Each day the promises of Jesus are that much closer for every one of us: "I will come back to take you with me." "I will be with you always, even until the end of time." "I am going to prepare a place for you." "This day you will be with me in Paradise."

Yes, joyful hope! The more we focus on these blessed things to come, the better we will be able to live as God intends us to live and thus the better prepared we will be to receive these gifts at the end of time. The day is ever nearer.

Bill Wack, C.S.C.

Monday, Week One

In days to come the mountain of the Lord's house shall be established as the highest of the mountains, and shall be raised above the hills; all the nations shall stream to it. Many peoples shall come and say, "Come, let us go up to the mountain of the Lord."

—Isaiah 2:2–3

WHEN IT CAME time for me to learn how to drive, I took lessons from the same instructor who taught my older siblings. He had one golden rule: "Keep your eyes up." He even had a mirror attached to the dashboard so that he could monitor from the passenger seat where we were looking with our eyes. He knew from years of experience that young drivers tend to focus on the road just in front of the car, thereby limiting their overall vision and not allowing for the proper perspective to see where they are headed.

His mantra of "keep your eyes up" is also a theme for these first days of Advent. The day-to-day busyness of our lives—the demands and pressures of work, school, family, and a host of other things—can easily cause us to lose the perspective that we are on a journey and that this world, while very important, is not our ultimate home. Yet we belong to God, and all of us are on a journey through this life to eternal life. That horizon, and the promise of eternal life that awaits us, is what gives meaning and purpose to all we do in this life. But it is a perspective we can easily lose sight of as we move through our days. Advent calls us to "keep our eyes up" and to remember that we are headed toward God's holy mountain to live in God's love forever.

Peter Jarret, C.S.C.

Tuesday, Week One

The wolf shall live with the lamb, the leopard shall lie down with the kid, the calf and the lion and the fatling together, and a little child shall lead them.

—Isaiah 11:6

As I walk down the hall of our nursing home, I wonder if this will be a good day for her. I see her sitting in her usual chair in the sunroom, gazing into space. I slowly approach, and her blue eyes meet mine. I tentatively reach out my arms and wait. This time I am rewarded. Her eyes light up; her arms open to me. I embrace her, and she whispers in my ear, "I am still waiting for Daddy. Will he come today?" I hug her tighter and respond, "He might come today. We will wait and see." In a bare whisper filled with intense emotion, she says, "Thank you. I love you." At that moment, all the conflicting forces of her dementia are at rest—the wolf and lamb, leopard and kid, calf and lion. There is peace. She settles back in the chair to continue her watchful vigil.

Advent invites us to embrace humbly and gratefully all the aspects of our inner life that are sometimes in conflict within us—our wolf and lamb, leopard and kid, calf and lion. Each one individually and all of them together are part of God's providential plan mysteriously at work within us. While held in God's loving embrace, we also yearn to be healed. Come, Lord Jesus, lead us and make us whole.

Mary Kay Kinberger, M.S.C.

Wednesday, Week One

He took the seven loaves and the fish; and after giving thanks he broke them and gave them to the disciples, and the disciples gave them to the crowds. And all of them ate and were

filled; and they took up the broken pieces left over, seven baskets full.
        —Matthew 15:36–37

DURING THE INSURGENCY in Northern Uganda, I lived with my parents in Congo as refugees for eight years. Every two weeks they would distribute food to the refugees. For us, the food was not only something to fill our hungry bellies, but also a tangible sign of hope. We were sure of living another day. Those distributions of food drew us refugees together and united us, giving us a common identity, as we faced the common problem of surviving away from our beloved country.

In today's gospel, Jesus miraculously feeds the crowd. With this miracle, Jesus seeks not merely to take away the people's physical hunger, but to give them hope—true hope that he, God-made-flesh, God-with-us, can take away their deepest hungers for forgiveness and healing, for justice and for peace . . . for God. And as he and his disciples distribute that sacrament of hope to the crowd, just as the priest and the ministers continue to distribute that sacrament of hope to us today in the Eucharist, Jesus draws us all together and unites us as one in our common identity as his brothers and sisters. Thus, nourished by him, we who are but pilgrims in this world, yearning for our heavenly homeland, become sure of living not just another day, but all eternity.

Comfort Agele, C.S.C.

Thursday, Week One

Everyone who hears these words of mine and acts on them will be like a wise man who built his house on rock. The rain fell, the floods came, and the winds blew and beat on that house, but it did not fall, because it had been founded on rock.

—Matthew 7:24–25

IT WAS NOT my habit to ask prisoners what they were in for. I only knew that Marcos was from the distant state of Ceará in northeast Brazil. When I offered him a New

Testament, he readily admitted: "Brother, I was only in the first grade for three months. I just learned the vowels." "Well," I responded, "ask for some help. Give it a try." One week later, grinning, he said, "Brother, I'm learning to read! I'm doing it!" And he told me who was helping him. Every week afterward, he would joyfully report his progress. When freed months later, he came to thank me before heading home by riverboat that night. He asked for nothing, but I was happy to be able to help him with a few clothes, a good meal, and a new New Testament.

Not to build our lives on rock is to risk disaster. Knowing that now, Marcos was sincerely grateful. He had read and now cherished the word. And the wonder of it all was that no other prisoner or guard had ever helped him. He said he knew that it was Jesus. We hope for that same faith to let Jesus teach us so our lives, too, may be founded on solid rock.

Harold Naudet, C.S.C.

Friday, Week One

I believe that I shall see the goodness of the Lord in the land of the living. Wait for the Lord, be strong, and let your heart take courage; wait for the Lord!

—Psalm 27:13–14

I HAVE HAD the privilege of serving as a spiritual companion to many economically poor people—people like Sarita in Monterrey, Mexico. Sarita made tortillas each day and then sold them. With the money she made from the tortillas, she would then buy food so that she could prepare a meal for her family. Sarita told me that she gave thanks to God for the strength to be able still to make tortillas after so many years and for the customers who purchased them. Sarita had found God in the land of the living—that is, in her daily life—and God never let her down. Her deep trust in Divine Providence gave her the courage to wait on the Lord. As a result, she was able to begin and face each new day with hope.

Sarita and other poor men and women like her have taught me that we really only have today and that God will provide us with what we need each day. Their example encourages all of us to wait on the Lord, to trust in Divine Providence on a daily basis. Then we, too, like them, will realize that the Lord is always worth the wait; he is always worth our trust.

Patricia Anne Clossey, C.S.C.

Saturday, Week One

As you go, proclaim the good news, "The kingdom of heaven has come near."

—Matthew 10:7

EVERY YEAR DURING Christmas, we go on a mission trip to Southern Chile with a group of our students from St. George's College in Santiago. It is a long journey of almost two days to a place where even the most basic amenities are left far behind. There are no cell phone towers, the closest electricity is miles away, and the only water available is what we can collect from the wells and streams and rain. Despite the rough conditions, we normally have over eighty young people who give fifteen days of their vacations to spread the joy, solidarity, and hope that Christ brings to the world.

As we prepare each year, we ask ourselves why we keep making the difficult trip. Yet once we arrive there, we remember right away how blessed it is to be invited by Christ to share his good news. It is amazing how our words, but above all our presence, can be a sign for the people that Christ himself has come to visit them. The smiles on their faces and the joy in their hearts as they welcome us into their simple homes far outweigh the small sacrifices we make in trying to reach them. And so it is every time we accept the Lord's call to be his missionary, for every time we let the Lord use us to bring his kingdom closer to others, we draw nearer to it ourselves.

José Ahumada, C.S.C.

Second Sunday

In those days John the Baptist appeared in the wilderness of Judea proclaiming, "Repent, for the kingdom of heaven has come near." This is the one of whom the prophet Isaiah spoke when he said, "The voice of one crying out in the wilderness: 'Prepare the way of the Lord, make his paths straight.'"

—Matthew 3:1–3

MAKING A PROCLAMATION, even a pointed one, is fine; the issue is whether or not anyone will pay attention. It becomes quickly evident that *what* is proclaimed cannot be conveniently or casually separated from *who* is proclaiming. The truth of the proclamation and the integrity of the preacher must be one and the same. There was no separation between John and his ministry and this explains why John the Baptist was such a powerful and probing preacher. His proclamation and way of life were one.

All in the family of Holy Cross are involved in a multitude of ministries around the world. The work for those ministries requires preparation and professionalism. Above all, however, it requires a quality of presence—a credibility and integrity that others will recognize and respect. Anything less would obscure the message being proclaimed. Even more, it could disrupt the very mission we are called to continue. Blessed Basil Moreau, our founder, believed that the personal quality of the minister, regardless of the work being done, was an essential apostolic force. He understood it to be the primary means by which we would communicate Jesus' message and continue his mission.

Whatever and wherever our work, we seek to call ourselves and others to new life by uniting our proclamation and our way of life as one. This, though, is a responsibility and a duty for all of us who are followers of Jesus. This is how we prepare for the Lord's coming; this is how we announce that the kingdom of heaven is near. John the

Baptist's summons to new life echoes today around the world in schools, parishes, hospitals, corporate offices, neighborhoods—wherever we, Christ's followers, are present. Our very lives are to inspire and draw others to prepare the way of the Lord. This is the heritage we share; this is the hope we bring.

Joel Giallanza, C.S.C.

Monday, Week Two

Strengthen the weak hands, and make firm the feeble knees. Say to those who are of a fearful heart, "Be strong, do not fear! Here is your God. . . ." Then the eyes of the blind shall be opened, and the ears of the deaf unstopped; then the lame shall leap like a deer, and the tongue of the speechless sing for joy.

—Isaiah 35:3–6

AFTER WORKING IN education for thirty years and then in campus ministry for another twenty, I am now in pastoral care at a retirement community. I am no longer teaching; I am the one being taught. Every day I see our residents with feeble hands, weak knees, limited sight, and hearing loss. And I watch them wait. They wait to be brought to their meals; they wait for their medicine; they wait to be helped to the bathroom. Most of them wait with great patience and a deep sense of gratitude.

One day, a jazz band came to entertain the residents. I watched in awe as crippled feet began to tap, weak knees slid back and forth, and bent shoulders rocked from side to side. Amazingly, as the music continued, feeble hands began to clap and worn out vocal chords to sing. That day God taught me a lesson about the beautiful kingdom to come. As we anxiously long for the fullness of that kingdom, we, too, can wait with great patience and a deep sense of gratitude because what God has promised, God is already beginning to fulfill. Yes, we can be strong, take courage, and fear not. The God we await, in many ways, is already in our midst.

Cynthia Knowles, M.S.C.

Tuesday, Week Two

If a shepherd has a hundred sheep, and one of them has gone astray, does he not leave the ninety-nine on the mountains and go in search of the one that went astray? And if he finds it, truly I tell you, he rejoices over it more than over the ninety-nine that never went astray.

—Matthew 18:12–13

SOME OF US who go astray are more easily identifiable than others. For example, in our diocese, we have a federal penitentiary, full of people who have gone astray. The justice system—and, for that matter, our society—classifies them as offenders and wants nothing to do with them. Yet my visits to detainees and my personal encounters with them have made me aware of how wounded they are and how they search for forgiveness and acceptance. No matter how badly they have behaved, they bear the marks of the Cross and show the face of Christ. They, too, are sheep of our flock, and they are certainly among those most in need. Through chaplains and other volunteers, our local church seeks to be present to those detainees and draw them back into the fold. As bishop of our diocese, I rejoice that we have so many searching out those in need of mercy and understanding.

A great part of being men and women with hope to bring is to reach out to one another when we have lost our way. Our hope is to be those men and women, preparing the way of the Lord in the lives of those who are lost so that we may all rejoice together at the coming of our Good Shepherd.

André Richard, C.S.C.

Wednesday, Week Two

Those who wait for the Lord shall renew their strength, they shall mount up with wings like eagles, they shall run and not be weary, they shall walk and not faint.

—Isaiah 40:31

ONE EVENING AFTER Mass in one of the chapels in our parish in Lima, Peru, a family asked me for a blessing. They were lighting candles before a painting of the crucifixion and touching their hands to the feet of Mary, John, and Jesus. After a brief invocation and making the Sign of the Cross over them, I stayed a moment to listen as the father told them that many in their family had found hope and real help by praying to Jesus, his best friend John, and his mother Mary, especially when they felt most helpless. He said that prayers before this painting were always answered and that was why they kept returning to it. Then they sang a short song, genuflected, and left. Once again, they had come asking for help, and once again, they left certain they would receive the miracle they needed.

That particular painting is called "The Lord of the Miracles," and for those in real need, that often is just who Jesus is. Our poor parish is filled with families who have an unwavering confidence in the Lord's power to work miracles in their lives and thus sustain them through all life's challenges and difficulties. Their faith and their devotions are a powerful witness that if we, too, can but have faith, the Lord shall renew our strength and we shall mount up with wings like eagles.

Robert Baker, C.S.C.

Thursday, Week Two

For I, the Lord your God, hold your right hand; it is I who say to you, "Do not fear, I will help you."

—Isaiah 41:13

WAITING CAN BE filled both with anticipation and, at times, with fear. A young man in my parish once told me that after he had crossed the border into Arizona, his "coyote"—a person who charges several thousand dollars to bring people across the border without papers—told him that the job he thought he had was not there. With no job and no money, the young man knew he could be either sent back or killed. He was flat-out scared as he waited in a sweltering hot shack in the Arizona desert. After an excruciating four days, his coyote told him that another family member had called with a job in Florida.

As we wait with anticipation this Advent for the coming of our Savior, we must remember our many brothers and sisters, like that young man, who wait and live with fear. Each day the millions of poor in our country and in our world desperately look for work and for food just to survive. It is a humiliating and frightening existence. It is an existence that challenges the rest of us to face and overcome our fears of getting involved with the poor and the marginalized, of reaching our hands out to them and saying together with the Lord, "Do not fear; I will help you."

Dan Kayajan, C.S.C.

Friday, Week Two

Thus says the Lord, your Redeemer, the Holy One of Israel: I am the Lord your God, who teaches you for your own good, who leads you in the way you should go.

—Isaiah 48:17

ONE WINTER EVENING, Rob was delivering flowers at a church. As he turned the truck around, he noticed something on the doorstep. When he went to investigate, he saw that it was a newborn baby and called 911. Medical personnel later said the baby was suffering from extreme hypothermia and would not have survived much longer in the cold. The local news media heard about Rob's quick action and came to interview the "hero" who saved the baby. When asked why he took action, he quickly responded, "At my school, they teach us to have the courage to act."

"St. Edward High School, a Catholic school in the Holy Cross tradition, educates the minds and hearts of young men to have the competence to see and the courage to act as men of faith." That is the mission statement of Rob's school. Rob accepted that mission and was ready to take action when it was needed. The mission was fulfilled.

We each must respond to God's call in our own lives. Sometimes, though, God uses us to be the instruments of his call to one another. The message and the mission are his, but we human beings are often

God's clearest voice, leading each other in the way we should go. It was good that Rob's teachers spoke with such a clear voice and that Rob was listening.

Kenneth Haders, C.S.C.

Saturday, Week Two

Turn again, O God of hosts; look down from heaven, and see; have regard for this vine, the stock that your right hand planted.

—Psalm 80:14–15

IN ONE OF the parishes where I worked as pastor in Bangladesh, there is a simple, uneducated man named Joseph Pereira. According to relatives, Joseph is 110 years old, although there is no official record of his date of birth. Even so, there is no doubt that Joseph is over 100 years old. He cannot see any more, but he still hears very clearly. And although he cannot walk, he still loves to talk to visitors. Every time relatives, friends, and villagers come to visit him, they express sympathy for him and his suffering at his old age. But once Joseph told me: "God is loving. He created me in his image. He gave me a long life and a happy family. I am grateful to him. He has taken care of me all these long years of my life, and he is going to do the same for the rest of my life. I always pray to God and I surrender myself to him, believing that if he has planted me in this world, he will also take care of me until the end."

Joseph's extraordinary faith and his total surrender to God were a great lesson for me. If a simple, uneducated man who has lived so long and suffered so much can entrust himself to the Lord's care and protection, so can we.

Boniface Tolentino, C.S.C.

Third Sunday

"Are you the one who is to come, or are we to wait for another?" Jesus

answered them, "Go and tell John what you hear and see: the blind receive their sight, the lame walk, the lepers are cleansed, the deaf hear, the dead are raised, and the poor have good news brought to them."

—Matthew 11:3–5

THIS QUESTION IS addressed to Jesus on behalf of John the Baptist, and there is a sense in which that is truly scandalous. After all, it was John who leaped in Elizabeth's womb when the mother of our Lord drew near. It was John who baptized Jesus and heard the voice from heaven say, "This is my beloved Son." It was John who pointed his disciples toward Jesus, saying, "Behold the Lamb of God!" How can it possibly be then that this same John asks Jesus if he is the one for whom the world has been waiting? We would love to have the kind of proofs John was given . . . and yet he doubts? What has changed? What has made John forget all he had once believed?

John sent his disciples to question Jesus from his prison cell where he awaited execution. He was facing a failure so complete that his life's glorious moments of clarity and faith seemed to have been negated. So perhaps we shouldn't be scandalized after all. In fact, maybe we can relate to how John must have felt. We, too, have had moments of clarity and faith when we were completely convinced of God's closeness and found it easy to believe. And then we have also had moments of doubt, when everything seemed to be going so completely wrong, that we found it nearly impossible to trust in God's promises.

In those moments we, like John, must reach the point where we discover God's love and closeness even in the darkness. This is true Advent hope. In the midst of nature's dark hours; in the midst of warfare and violence, poverty and natural disasters; in the midst of our own sinfulness and failures the season of Advent reminds us that even through suffering and death Jesus is still Emmanuel, God-with-us, until the end of the ages.

Stephen M. Koeth, C.S.C.

Monday, Week Three

Be mindful of your mercy, O Lord, and of your steadfast love, for they have been from of old.

—Psalm 25:6

ONE DAY IN Ghana an older student brought a young boy to see me. He was away from home for the first time and was apparently having some difficulty adjusting. I asked him what was wrong. "I can't sleep at night," he responded. "Why not?" I asked. "My grandmother keeps coming to visit me." I found out that his grandmother had died just two months ago. I then asked, "Is she coming to harm you?" "Oh no, she's protecting me." He went on to say that if he didn't get his sleep soon his studies would suffer. I gave him a rosary and told him to say one Hail Mary and then ask Jesus to tell his grandmother that he liked to see her but that he needed his sleep. She never bothered him again.

In Africa, ancestors are God's special guardians; they are signs of his steadfast love. I could have told this young man to wake up, that there are no ghosts; instead, I learned something. Since then, I have prayed every day to my ancestors to protect and guide me. Now they have become signs to me, as they can be to all of us, that God's steadfast love is nothing new—that it truly is from of old.

Raymond Papenfuss, C.S.C.

Tuesday, Week Three

"Truly I tell you, the tax collectors and the prostitutes are going into the kingdom of God ahead of you. For John came to you in the way of righteousness and you did not believe him, but the tax collectors and the prostitutes believed him. . . ."

—Matthew 21:31–32

IF I WERE to paint the kingdom of God, I would use the best canvas. Vibrant and rich colors would swirl in dancing lines. Balance and harmony would rule, bringing pleasure to the eyes. Only a professional would be worthy to frame it. But if this is a true vision of the kingdom proclaimed by Jesus, why would tax collectors and prostitutes enter this well-ordered world before me? Perhaps it is because life has taught them to live with lines that are not so clearly defined. Life has challenged them to dance to unexpected and less than harmonious music, and as a result, their hearts are more open to God.

This reality might lead us to examine the openness of our own hearts, those canvases upon which the Spirit yearns to paint freely with lines often unfamiliar to us. Opening our hearts might make us relinquish our neat and comfortable way of living. It might force us hear our chaotic world pleading for voices to speak out boldly against injustice and inequality. Dare we let our hearts hear and follow the Spirit into these marginal spaces? Dare we let our souls rise up with courage and respond? To be a true disciple of God's kingdom asks no less of us. For truly Jesus tells us, the Kingdom of God is made of these.

Therese Fortin, C.S.C.

Wednesday, Week Three

Shower, O heavens, from above, and let the skies rain down righteousness; let the earth open, that salvation may spring up, and let it cause righteousness to sprout up also; I the Lord have created it.

—Isaiah 45:8

IN MY SIXTEEN years in Lima, it rained once. Most of the coast of Peru is a desert, and Lima, a city of eight million, is in the middle of it. How I would long for a good rainstorm to wash everything clean—as I would long much more intensely for righteousness to rain down in our world so in need of a cleansing of injustice, corruption, and poverty. Yet these words of Isaiah are not his prayer; they are God's command: I the Lord have created it. God is saying he will do it.

The one time it rained in Lima was a disaster. Thousands were left homeless as torrents ran off the hillsides and washed away their poorly built shacks. I came to appreciate the fog that would settle over the coastal region with its gentle mist. Similarly, over the years, I have pondered what it means that the Kingdom of God arrived in one baby born in a stable and destined to die on a cross. That's not the downpour of righteousness I might imagine in my dreams, yet it is how God works. God casts down the mighty and lifts up the lowly. God does wonders and is mindful of his promises. Yet he does so through humble servants who, like Mary, find joy in saying yes to life, to love, to truth, to peace—through those who follow Christ as he redeems the world by bringing life out of death through love.

Jim Phalan, C.S.C.

Thursday, Week Three

For the mountains may depart and the hills be removed, but my steadfast love shall not depart from you, and my covenant of peace shall not be removed, says the Lord, who has compassion on you.

—Isaiah 54:10

AS A RELIGIOUS sister ministering with young people, I am often challenged with questions like: "Why does God let this happen?" or "Why doesn't God stop that?" or "Where is God in this?" My faith tells me that God's covenant of peace is not necessarily a promise of perfection—that all will be right in this world—but rather a promise of presence—that in the midst of what is in this world, God will always and everywhere be present.

In the aftermath of Hurricane Katrina, however, I joined the masses who struggled to answer for ourselves those same questions.

But the answer came: God was there. God was there in the people offering hospitality and a meal in the evacuation shelters. God was there in the National Guard and the first responders who risked their lives to bring a sense of normalcy to the city. God was there in the call from a friend, the text message of a family member, a gift card from a stranger. In very real ways, God was present in the little, ordinary miracles sent our way just to let us know we were not alone in our struggle. God was there.

As we weather the storms in our daily lives, we seek the comfort of knowing that God's covenant of peace is, indeed, a promise of presence, of steadfast love, and of compassion for all people.

Keri Burke, M.S.C.

Friday, Week Three

My house shall be called a house of prayer for all peoples. Thus says the Lord God, who gathers the outcasts of Israel, I will gather others to them besides those already gathered.
—Isaiah 56:7–8

I LIVE NOT far from a basilica in Bangalore, India, dedicated to Our Lady of Good Health. On Christmas 2008, I visited the basilica late in the evening to avoid the rush. To my surprise, the church was still packed. Barefoot and kneeling as they approached the sanctuary, the people, with unmistakable prayers on their lips, held lit candles and gazed expectantly at the immaculate face of our Mother and her Child. Most of them were Muslims and Hindus, who, according to the pastor, were the remnant of the estimated fifty-five thousand people who visited the church that day.

How true it is that the Lord in his own way gathers all others into his fold! As we await his coming, we are challenged to discover the myriad of ways in which the Lord offers to bring people into his house. And still we are caught unaware. In my own ministry at our school, I have come to know that so many children and parents have an unexplainable yearning and an unquenchable thirst for something greater, regardless of their religious allegiance. Especially in the face of growing religious intolerance and fundamentalism, it is essential for us to be agents of interreligious dialogue and so let the Lord be revealed in the hearts of many who do not know him who was born in Bethlehem—for all people.

John Britto, C.S.C.

Fourth Sunday

All this took place to fulfill what had been spoken by the Lord through the prophet: "Look, the virgin shall

conceive and bear a son, and they shall name him Emmanuel," which means, "God is with us."
—Matthew 1:22–23

A CHILD IS Christmas shopping with his mother. They walk through aisle after aisle of toys. He lets go of her hand to run after something shiny on a low shelf. Fascinated by what he has found, he has no attention to spare for the world around him. After who knows how long, he decides to show the newfound treasure to his mother. He looks up. She's not here. He calls for her. No reply. The bottom falls out of his world. He's alone and terribly afraid.

Most of us can remember when something like this happened to us. Maybe the fear, once felt, never really goes away. All our waking lives we hurry from one distraction to another. And when no external diversions are at hand, we lavish mental energy on mind games of embarrassing triviality. Why do we behave this way? Could it be that long years after our first traumatic childhood experience, we are still haunted by the suspicion that if we look up from the things that divert us, we will find we have been left alone again, this time forever, in an uncaring, unheeding world? So, afraid of what we might see if we look life in the eye, we cling to our distractions and waste our precious lives, failing to live and love as we should.

Luke proclaims to us the great good news that we need not be afraid, because in Jesus Christ, God is with us. "God is with us." Can I feel the deep comfort in those words? God is with me, so that even when I feel most alone, I am a "we." And there is nothing that we need fear, no one that we cannot love.

Charles B. Gordon, C.S.C.

December 17

. . . and Eliud the father of Eleazar, and Eleazar the father of Matthan, and Matthan the father of Jacob, and Jacob the father of Joseph the

husband of Mary, of whom Jesus was
born, who is called the Messiah.
—Matthew 1:15–16

I CAME TO Holy Cross largely because of the example of two priests—my great-uncle and my brother. They showed such faith and joy in their ministries that I could not help but be drawn to the community. I am privileged now to carry on our family name within the family of Holy Cross.

Just like Jesus, we are all born into a family at a particular time and a particular place. None of us are arbitrarily chosen. "Before I formed you in the womb, I knew you," the Lord tells us (Jer 1:5). Of course, God not only knew us before we were born, but he also knew our families. And so God knows that we do not come from perfect families—but neither did Jesus. In his genealogy, there are both great sinners as well as great saints.

What makes people saintly, ourselves included, is not that we or our families are perfect, but rather that we seek day after day to be more like Jesus Christ by living and loving as he did. In doing so, we certainly try to draw upon the examples of holiness we find in our own families, but we also draw upon the examples of holiness we find in our brothers and sisters in Christ. For each of us is part of that greater family, God's family, called to reflect the light and the love of Jesus Christ to the world.

Neil Wack, C.S.C.

December 18

Her husband Joseph, being a righteous man and unwilling to expose her to public disgrace, planned to dismiss her quietly. But just when he had resolved to do this, an angel of the Lord appeared to him in a dream. . . . When Joseph awoke from sleep, he did as the angel of the Lord commanded him. . . .

—Matthew 1:19–20, 24

WHILE REFLECTING RECENTLY on the birth of Jesus, I was struck by how little thought I had given to St. Joseph over the years in my reflections on that amazing event. I had even been to Bethlehem and visited the place where Jesus was born on several occasions due to my work. But in all those visits and in all those reflections, I never really paid any attention to Joseph. In my thoughts, it was as if he was just there. In that moment of insight, however, I realized that Joseph was not just there. Like Mary and really like everyone else gathered around the newborn babe in the manger, Joseph was there because God willed him to be there. Joseph, just like Mary, was doing God's will. It was his yes, just like Mary's, that had allowed this miracle to take place.

Joseph's righteousness was that he did not allow what other people would think of him or say about him to prevent him from doing what God had commanded him. In standing properly before God, he was able to be right where God—and others—needed him to be. We pray for that same righteousness, that same strength of character so that we can be right where the Lord needs us to be

. . . even if in the end others might think we are just there.

James E. McDonald, C.S.C.

December 19

After those days his wife Elizabeth conceived, and for five months she remained in seclusion. She said, "This is what the Lord has done for me when he looked favorably on me and took away the disgrace I have endured among my people."

—Luke 1:24–25

FOR WOMEN IN Bangladesh, barrenness is a source of great disgrace, humiliation, and suffering. In both Bengali and tribal cultures here, a married woman is not really welcomed into the family until she gives birth. If she fails to bear a child, often the husband and his family blame her. Others in society criticize her as well. Not surprisingly, many childless women become depressed, hopeless in a way, running from one shrine to another, one doctor to another, seeking relief from this disgrace. Like Elizabeth, some women eventually conceive, sometimes many years later, and experience God's grace through the extraordinary birth of their child. This child then becomes the source of peace and happiness in their lives and in their families.

Barrenness, however, is not limited just to a lack of children. Many of us wrestle with other forms of barrenness—and the shame and suffering that come with them—as we struggle to bear fruit in our lives, whether that be at school or at work, in our ministries or in our relationships with others. This Advent season we look once again with expectant and joyful hope to the coming of our Lord, praying that his birth in our lives will remove any disgrace through his holy grace.

Minoti Rozario, C.S.C.

December 20

Then Mary said, "Here am I, the servant of the Lord; let it be with me according to your word."

—Luke 1:38

MARY'S "YES" TO the Angel Gabriel and to the invitation to be the Mother of God has inspired countless men and women over the centuries to give their own yes to God. I know in my own life that it is Mary's *fiat* that has given me the courage to say yes to the Lord, especially when it has been uncertain where my yes would lead me. Mary herself did not know everything that being the mother of Jesus would require of her, but how could she know? How could she know that her son would be a sign that would be contradicted? How could she know that her heart would be pierced seven times? The angel never told her that.

Similarly, how are we to know all that our yes to the Lord will demand of us? Like

Mary, we cannot know. When I said yes to the priesthood, I never thought I would become the president of the University of Notre Dame or serve on the civil rights commission or do so many other things I have done as a Holy Cross priest. And yet, just like with Mary, God is waiting for our yes. Drawing inspiration from our mother, Mary, we seek the courage to respond with her, "Here we are, Lord; let it be done to us according to your word."

Theodore M. Hesburgh, C.S.C.

December 21

When Elizabeth heard Mary's greeting, the child leaped in her womb. And Elizabeth was filled with the Holy Spirit and exclaimed with a loud cry, "Blessed are you among women, and blessed is the fruit of your womb."

—Luke 1:41–42

AS I LISTEN to Elizabeth's greeting of Mary, I am reminded of the common greeting here in Uganda: "You are *most* welcome!" Whenever I hear it, I feel something within me jump for joy. It reminds me of a visit we made to the home of Edith, one of our candidates in formation to become a sister. We had driven all day on a road that hardly qualified as a road. In fact, I kept asking our guide if we were going the right way. As we made the final turn, we came face to face with a large tree in the middle of the road, that was now really nothing more than a path. As we sat there, surveying the situation and our options, several young men appeared from Edith's home with *pangas* and axes to clear the way. We were truly "*most* welcome."

Welcoming others into our lives is not always easy. Often, it is a lot easier to keep others at a distance. Yet how can we ever hope to welcome Jesus if we cannot welcome our brothers and sisters in him? These final days before Christmas are a good time for us to reflect on what obstacles and barriers we have erected to prevent others from getting close to us, so that we might then clear the way for them and for Jesus to be *most* welcome in our lives.

Mary Louise Wahler, C.S.C.

December 22

And Mary said, "My soul magnifies the Lord, and my spirit rejoices in God my Savior, for he has looked with favor on the lowliness of his servant. Surely, from now on all generations will call me blessed. . . ."

—Luke 1:46–48

As a young woman, I dreamt of when I would be a nun, given totally to God. When I gave my yes to God, however, little did I know—much like Mary—how my life would actually unfold. I was not prepared, or so I thought, to give the gift that would be asked of me—my health.

Multiple sclerosis became part of my life over thirty years ago at age thirty-four. I slowly lost my ability to walk and to do

things with my hands, becoming perma-
nently confined to a wheelchair. What I had
thought it meant to be productive was no
longer possible. I could have become angry,
bitter, and resentful; instead, by God's grace,
I was able to give a yes that truly took my
life out of my hands. With that yes, the
Spirit has guided me through MS down
pathways I would not have chosen myself.
Along the way, I have received insight and
wisdom with which to recognize God's voice
within myself and within those I encounter.
Through hearing their suffering, pain, and
anguish, I try to help them discover the gift
of who they are and who they are meant to
be, because it is when we say yes to who we
really are that our spirits rejoice in God our
Savior and we are truly blessed.

Cecile Paquette, C.S.C.

December 23

*See, I am sending my messenger to
prepare the way before me, and the*

Lord whom you seek will suddenly come to his temple. The messenger of the covenant in whom you delight—indeed, he is coming, says the Lord of hosts.

—Malachi 3:1

ALTHOUGH I AM not always aware of them, God's messengers are many in my life. They are the beggar whom I meet unexpectedly, but whose request brings out the best in me; the dear friend whom I have not seen for a long time, but who calls me on my birthday; the coworker who, noticing my weariness, offers to take me home at the end of a long day. When I actually take the time and reflect on what their presence really means in my life, these and many others become for me the messengers God intended them to be. For often such reflection becomes a spark that reawakens my faith to see their presence as God's presence, proclaiming to me the good news that the Lord is near.

In these hectic days before Christmas, many of us probably have been busy with so many things that we have not been attentive enough to the people God has been sending to remind us: "I am coming, for you and for all my people." So even though we still have so much to do to get ready for Christmas, perhaps the most important thing we can do is nothing at all. Simply stop and reflect on the messengers God has sent us to prepare his way in our lives again this Christmas. For, indeed, he is coming.

Gérard Dionne, C.S.C.

December 24—Christmas Eve

The people who walked in darkness have seen a great light; those who lived in a land of deep darkness—on them light has shined. . . . For a child has been born for us, a son given to us; authority rests upon his shoulders; and he is named Wonderful Counselor, Mighty God, Everlasting Father, Prince of Peace.

—Isaiah 9:2, 6

WE IN HOLY Cross profess to be men and women with hope to bring. Wonderful! Yet, what can this mean when, as humans, we must spend part of our lives in Isaiah's deep darkness? As mere humans, we all must spend parts of our lives in doubt, loneliness, or suffering. Given this reality, how can we call ourselves a people with hope to bring? In times of darkness, symbolized by these late December days, what allows us to be bearers of hope?

To be true Advent people we must recognize this reality: it is not the facts of our human existence that give us reason to hope. The facts of our human weakness—our blindness, the power of evil, darkness— threaten to overwhelm us. How then can we be bearers of hope? How, but through a gift, the very gift which we long to receive in these last Advent days? A gift offered by God into our human lives, the gift of hope?

We are, indeed, a people with hope to bring. This hope is not self-generated or dependent on the often-dark facts of our lives. We are a people with hope to bring because we are recipients of a divine gift— the gift of Christmas—which invites us to believe that the darkness in our world is not the final fact. God has stirred our hearts with the gift of hope! This hope awakens us to the possibility that tomorrow light will shine in our darkness. May we be ever more open to this Christmas gift, the light of a Mighty God and Prince of Peace. May we be vessels of his light and messengers of Good News—a people with hope to bring!

Lou DelFra, C.S.C.

December 25—Christmas Day

While [Joseph and Mary] were [in Bethlehem], the time came for her to deliver her child. And she gave birth to her firstborn son and wrapped him in bands of cloth, and laid him in a manger, because there was no place for them in the inn.

—Luke 2:6–7

I ONCE HAD the rare opportunity to spend Christmas in Bethlehem celebrating midnight

Mass at the famed Church of the Nativity. I anticipated it to be the highlight of my time in this Holy Land. To my utter disappointment and disillusionment, what I actually experienced that night was a carnival atmosphere of crowds pushing and shoving. I was exhausted due to the late hour and the day's full schedule, and I longed to be home in a familiar place with those I loved. "Where was Emmanuel, God-with-me?" I wondered that night.

For centuries, the people of Israel clung to their expectations of the promised Savior. They anticipated an earthly king who would save them from their enemies, expel their Roman occupiers, and make their tiny nation important and prosperous. What came instead was an infant born in a stable— a countercultural, itinerant preacher who challenged religious authorities, destabilized the prevailing norm of who was valued, and suffered and died on a cross. "How could this be the promised Emmanuel, God-with-us?" they had to wonder.

Our expectations of what Christmas will be like may also get shattered as the reality unfolds. We anticipate and long for the warmth of family and friendship, peace on earth, and the joy of the heralding angels. Instead of this idyllic picture, Christmas sometimes arrives with broken hearts and relationships, a weary world at war, and the cries of the poor drowning out the heralding angels. "Where is our Emmanuel, God-with-us?" we wonder.

God's desire to be with us was expressed totally in the human flesh of Jesus. That same desire to be with us is poured into our own flesh in an abiding presence and promise beyond our greatest expectations or our deepest disillusionments. This is the God-with-us that we celebrate today and carry into the world.

Mary Ellen Vaughan, C.S.C.

Holy Family—Sunday after Christmas

When [the Holy Family] had finished everything required by the law of the Lord, they returned to Galilee, to their own town of Nazareth. The

child grew and became strong, filled
with wisdom. . . .

—Luke 2:39–40

JOSEFINA AND RAUL were expecting baby number six when I first met them. That day, Raul was out looking for work in the sprawling city of Monterrey in northern Mexico. Two of their children, Raulito and Maria, had gone to accompany their grandmother to ensure she would arrive safely to their one-room home while the others remained at home. Josefina was preparing lunch while Edgar and Julio played quietly in the corner. Four-year-old Cynthia sang and danced around the room. Even though she had just been in the hospital due to complications with her pregnancy, Josefina could not wait to welcome her mother-in-law into her home for the day. As I sat on the only chair in the house and looked at the old, lumpy sofa where several of the children slept and the one bed that the rest of them had to share, my heart was profoundly touched by the holiness of this family. Their willingness to share what little they had spoke of a deep trust in Divine Providence that still inspires me.

Families must deal with many forces that make it difficult to spend quality time together. Work schedules, school, sports, dance and music lessons, as well as time out with friends all compete with the need simply to sit down together and share a meal. And then, even when we are together, many of us, both young and not so young, have some kind of gadget plugged into our ears or held in our hands. We in Holy Cross, whose founder was inspired by the image of the Holy Family, are not immune to this struggle either, with our often hectic lives and penchant for multitasking. Today's feast reminds us how important it is for families to set aside time for relating in a deeply personal way. Every family is called to be a place where each member can grow and become strong. Every family is invited to share in God's life of grace. Every family is called to be a holy family.

Carola LeBoeuf, M.S.C.

December 26—St. Stephen

Then they dragged [Stephen] out of the city and began to stone him; and the witnesses laid their coats at the feet of a young man named Saul. While they were stoning Stephen, he prayed, "Lord Jesus, receive my spirit."

—Acts 7:58–59

YESTERDAY WE CELEBRATED Jesus' birth. Today we celebrate the birth into eternal life of one of his earliest followers, Saint Stephen. Stephen, the first martyr in the church, was an example of a true Christian. He witnessed to Jesus in a bold and fearless way, even laying down his life for him. History is replete with Christians who have died witnessing to the faith, but martyrdom is not just a thing of the past. Many Christians in our day continue to face persecution and pay the ultimate price of their lives—Christians like Rakesh Digal, a young Catholic from the state of Orissa in India. He was on vacation in his village when a roaming Hindu mob spotted him. He tried to run away but was caught. He was beaten and buried alive for refusing to renounce his faith. When he asked why they were burying him alive, the Hindu assailants told him, "Jesus will save you."

Martyrs like Stephen and Rakesh remind us that following the Lord demands the readiness to lay down our lives for him. Their witness and sacrifice inspire us to follow Jesus without compromise in our own lives. After all, to give us birth into eternal life, Jesus was not just born as one of us, he also died for us.

Lumen Monteiro, C.S.C.

December 27—St. John, Apostle and Evangelist

We declare to you what was from the beginning, what we have heard, what we have seen with our eyes,

what we have looked at and touched
with our hands, concerning the word
of life—this life was revealed, and we
have seen it and testify to it.
                                        —1 John 1:1–2

FRESH FROM MY seminary studies at the University of Notre Dame, I was participating in a meeting of Holy Cross men in formation and vocation work. They asked me to describe briefly my experience as a deacon over the preceding months. Reflecting on it in light of my recent theological studies, I explained that, ultimately, I understood my ministry as that of being a sacrament of God's love. Moments later, a seminarian living at my parish introduced himself, saying with a mischievous grin on his face, "I live with the sacrament of God's love!" Everyone had a good laugh, myself included, but clearly they had been listening and gotten my point.

The Christmas season calls us to live out in our daily lives the reality of God's incarnate love. Others should see in us incarnations of the Incarnation, able to hear and see and know God's love through us.

Indeed, we must be for others sacraments of God's presence, testifying with our lives to the word of life, Jesus of Nazareth, through which we have come to know the fullness of life.

Jim Fenstermaker, C.S.C.

December 28—Holy Innocents

When Herod saw that he had been tricked by the wise men, he was infuriated, and he sent and killed all the children in and around Bethlehem who were two years old or under. . . .

—Matthew 2:16

ONE CHRISTMAS MORNING, as we were opening our church for our first Mass, a member of our Spanish choir came and told me that the choir would not be able to perform that morning. I had a heart attack! No music on Christmas?! I took a breath and asked what the problem was.

The gentleman told me that during the night the infant grandson of the couple who leads the choir had died. I immediately rushed to their home and found a house full of people wailing and crying. The child's grandmother told me that her grandson had been sleeping in bed with his parents. Somehow during the night, one of them had rolled over on the four-month-old baby and suffocated him. How could this be? How could God allow such a horrible thing to happen on Christmas day?

Today's remembrance of the Holy Innocents can provoke a similar question in us: How could God allow King Herod to slaughter those innocent children? We simply do not know. But we do know this—that the same Son of God who came as Emmanuel, God-with-us, remained with us through his own senseless suffering and death on the Cross to reveal to us in his resurrection that God's love for us is stronger than death. That's not an answer to that baby's death; it's not an explanation to any of this world's tragedies. But it is a love that transcends all our questions, all our tears, all our suffering; it is a love that lasts forever.

John Herman, C.S.C.

December 29

Then Simeon blessed them and said to his mother Mary, "This child is destined for the falling and the rising of many in Israel, and to be a sign that will be opposed so that the inner thoughts of many will be revealed— and a sword will pierce your own soul too."

—Luke 2:34–35

I WONDER WHAT was going through Mary's mind and heart as she heard Simeon's words predicting future suffering for her son and for herself. The angel Gabriel had said, "Don't be afraid, Mary. . . . The Holy Spirit will come upon you and the power of the Most High will overshadow you. . . . Nothing is impossible with God." These words did not seem to indicate that a sword would pierce her soul. Was Mary—Our Lady of Sorrows—able to respond with the same "let it be done to me as you say" that she had given at the annunciation?

Many times in my life I have responded with an enthusiastic "yes" to a request of my community, ministry, family, or friends. All seems fine, even exciting at first. Then life happens, difficulties arise, doubts surface, and I question my ability to do what is needed. My yes is no longer filled with my initial enthusiasm; rather, fear, hesitancy, and questioning begin to take over. This is not what I had in mind, I think to myself. But when I can recall that nothing is impossible with God, peace once again returns.

I am sure Mary remembered God's promise, and this gave her the courage to say yes again and again through all her joys and her sorrows. And it is remembering God's promise that gives us the grace and the strength to say yes too.

Suellen Tennyson, M.S.C.

December 30

Do not love the world or the things in the world. The love of the Father is not in those who love the world. . . . And the world and its desire are passing away, but those who do the will of God live forever.

—1 John 2:15, 17

WITH THE DECORATIONS still hanging and gifts hopefully given and received and still very fondly thought of, our scriptures tell us not to love the world or the things in the world. We remain in the octave of Christmas, the celebration of God loving the world so much that he sent his only Son into it. Yet our scriptures also say that the love of the Father is not in those who love the world.

Perhaps there is a key to resolving this apparent discrepancy. Whether I have been in studies, working in a parish, or working among people who are homeless and often struggling with addictions, the truth of both sides has been clear. When God created the world, God proclaimed that it was good. Yet too often we can get caught in love with the world and we forget the Creator, worshipping the gifts and not the Giver. Whether a person is homeless or a multimillionaire, the truth remains that the things of the world will pass away. When we love the things of the world, we end up with nothing but the transitory. But when we choose to follow God's example, when we choose to love the people of this world, we have everything.

Eric Schimmel, C.S.C.

December 31

And the Word became flesh and lived among us, and we have seen his glory, the glory as of a father's only son, full of grace and truth. . . . From his fullness we have all received, grace upon grace.

—John 1:14, 16

SINCE I WAS a child, I have been fascinated by all the people in the story of the birth of the baby of Bethlehem, Jesus. Multitudes of heavenly hosts are singing, "Glory to God in the highest!" Shepherds are running excitedly to the stable. Mary and Joseph, young parents completely open to God's will, bask in the beauty of the newborn child. Magi from the East—exotic, learned, and wealthy—follow a star. In his poem "Star of the Nativity," Joseph Brodsky even imagines the star "from the depths of universe, from its opposite end" as "looking into the cave."

There are more than enough exciting characters in this wondrous story to capture any imagination. In fact, at different moments in our lives, we probably identify more closely with different characters and their particular experiences of Christ's miraculous birth. They linger in our mind's eyes and dwell in our hearts. Their stories inspire us to tell of our own experience of the Word, who is Love, becoming flesh and living among us in our own lives. In that way, we join our voices to theirs in testifying to the world that we, indeed, have seen his glory and thereby have received grace upon grace.

Thomas A. Dziekan, C.S.C.

January 1—Mary, Mother of God

But Mary treasured all these words and pondered them in her heart.
—Luke 2:19

IN MY MINISTRY I facilitate women's retreats and faith-sharing groups. When we do a sharing of an experience of God's presence in our lives, very often a woman describes the birth of her child as a profound experience of awe and of the sacred. I could imagine that Mary had a similar experience with the birth of her son, Jesus. Words to describe the miracle of the birth of one's child are hard to come by. For Mary, pondering this in her heart was a way for her to keep returning to it and thus to treasure its richness evermore.

At these retreats, I congratulate the women gathered for taking this "pause time" from their busy lives. Social and peer pressure exist to keep us busy caring for others. As important as it is to care for others, however, there is a balance needed. Whether women or men, we need time to treasure an experience of the holy. We need to get beyond the guilt of taking time for ourselves in this manner and learn to distinguish between selfishness and self-care. As we begin to do so, giving ourselves the pauses we need to ponder and treasure life, we become empowered to live with a new depth in our hearts.

Not all of us are birth mothers, but we all have moments of the sacred. It could be a magnificent sunset over the ocean, a tiny crocus coming up through the snow, or a time of prayer touching our hearts. From my experience, a good time to pause is the evening when we can ponder over the events of the day. Small moments can take on new meaning as gifts of the sacred. We can even be surprised by the gift hidden in some mishap or cross. If we pause and look more deeply, we will find that life gives us countless occasions that when treasured and pondered lead us deeper into the mystery of Emmanuel, God-with-us. Mary, our mother, has given us an example.

Patricia Cornell, C.S.C.

January 2

All the ends of the earth have seen the victory of our God. Make a joyful noise to the Lord, all the earth; break forth into joyous song and sing praises.

—Psalm 98:3–4

To be Christian is to live in song. When I sing God's praises, despite my lack of vocal talent, I know I am living out a certain truth of what it is to be Christian. For us, wonders have never ceased; dreams can still come true. Our being hopeful is a genuine stance toward a world all too pessimistic. So powerful are the miracles of the Incarnation and the resurrection that their sheer impossibility throws into question what we human beings think is possible. The reality that God could become human and that a man could be raised from the dead just do not compute in our logic-driven world.

Yet in the face of such unbelief, we Christians continue to sing God's praises. And we do so understanding that this singing does nothing really—that is, it does not build bridges, it does not cause electricity to flow into our homes, it does not even accrue wealth for us. There is no useful societal good produced when we sing God's praises. Yet this is just where we need to be. In song, we are beholden to no political party, no cult of personality, no newfangled fanaticism that seems to enrapture the public all too often. In song, we are joined together in a crescendo of joy that will resound through the heavens. In song, we are a tangible sign of God's abundant love.

Paul Ybarra, C.S.C.

January 3

See what love the Father has given us, that we should be called children of God; and that is what we are.

—1 John 3:1

THE YOUNG MEN and women who attend our universities usually strike me as so "put together." Their physical appearance, their dress, and the way they can articulate their knowledge and life experience lures me into assuming that the next generation has transcended the problems of our world and that they have a clear course of action for building the kingdom of God. During my first Christmas break in the dorm, however, a day after all students were supposed to have vacated, I ran across one of these "put together" students hiding in the hall. My initial instinct was to reprimand him for his violation. I was wrong. In subsequent hours, listening to his story, I learned that he did not want to go home. His home was a chaotic, violent place.

Try as they might, none of our parents are perfect, nor can we expect them to be. They, like us, are often not as put together as they would want to be. Our awareness of ourselves as children of God can be both enlightened and obscured by our experience of being children of our parents. Yet, as children of God, the Father does not reprimand us for our shortcomings or violations; nor does he chasten imperfect parents. See what love the Father has given us, as he sits patiently and listens to us tell our story.

Thomas Doyle, C.S.C.

January 4

When Jesus turned and saw them following, he said to them, "What are you looking for?" They said to him, "Rabbi" (which translated means Teacher), "where are you staying?" He said to them, "Come and see."

They came and saw where he was staying.

—John 1:38–39

WHILE IN THE seminary, I was given this passage for meditation. The idea was to place myself in the scene and imagine what it would be like to stand before Jesus as he asked, "What are you looking for?" It was powerful to imagine myself before Christ with the opportunity to interact with him. As I did so, I realized that if anyone had the answers to the questions weighing upon me, he was the one. So I placed my concerns before him: What is it that you are asking of me? Is it really priesthood and religious life? How am I to be sure I am following your call?

More stirring than the opportunity to unburden myself was the answer that came: "Come and see." That answer did not relieve me of the need to wrestle with the question of my call as I had hoped, but it did relieve the pressure I felt to figure it out right then. That moment of prayer gave me the peace to know that the answers I sought would come in time. In the meantime, I simply had to follow Christ and remain open to where he led. And that, quite often, is the answer for many of us in our different life situations. The discernment of our call frequently does not come in a flash of revelation, but through time spent seeking to know, love, and serve Christ more fully.

James Gallagher, C.S.C.

January 5

We know that we have passed from death to life because we love one another. Whoever does not love abides in death. . . . We know love by this, that he laid down his life for us—and we ought to lay down our lives for one another.

—1 John 3:14, 16

ONE AFTERNOON AT Holy Cross Ministries in Salt Lake City, Aniceto, Esperanza, and Alma were closing down the after-school program and rounding up children for the bus, when Aniceto spied a fifth-grader standing off to the side. "Come here, *campeón*!" he called out to the young boy. He then began to brag of the boy's achievements in the pickup soccer game that day. Everyone complimented him and promised to swing by the field the next day to catch a glimpse of his skills. As the group dispersed, the boy lingered, so Aniceto asked, "What are you thinking, *campeón*?" The boy replied, "You seem like you like to be with us." Taken aback briefly, Aniceto said, "Of course I like to be with you!"

If there is one thing that we all long for in our lives, it is one another. We long for an act of welcome, a word of affirmation, an invitation to belong. We, like that boy, are looking for others who want to be with us. When we talk about laying down our lives for one another, however, it can seem that simply wanting to be with one another does not really count. It is not sacrifice enough. Yet that often is how love really starts. After all, before he laid down his life for us, Jesus simply desired to become one of us and be one with us.

Mary Ann Pajakowski, C.S.C.

January 6—Epiphany and Blessed Brother André

When [the wise men] saw that the star had stopped, they were overwhelmed with joy. On entering the house, they saw the child with Mary his mother; and they knelt down and paid him homage. Then, opening their treasure chests, they offered him gifts of gold, frankincense, and myrrh.

—Matthew 2:10–11

TODAY IS THE twelfth day of Christmas, the day we traditionally celebrate the feast of the Epiphany, commemorating the wise men who followed the star to give homage to the newborn Christ Child. They came bearing him gifts: gold, symbolizing the power and wealth of a king; frankincense, which gives tribute to what is holy; and myrrh, an ointment to anoint the sick and the dying.

The church has also reserved this day to celebrate the Feast of Blessed Brother André Bessette, C.S.C., the founder of St. Joseph's Oratory in Montreal, Quebec. What a joy it is for Holy Cross to celebrate one of its saints on this special day! His appearance and demeanor were far from regal, yet in his humility and loving compassion for the sick, Brother André commanded of those who had the privilege of meeting him the respect and honor fit for a king. Similar to the Magi, Brother André in his own faith journey presented to the Lord his own special gifts. Although his religious poverty prevented him from giving gold, he generously gave of his own personal treasure of profound faith and healing to the thousands who came to see him. In many ways his frankincense was the dream and construction of the oratory itself, a striking memorial honoring the holiness of his beloved St. Joseph. And finally, his myrrh was the holy oil he used in his ministry to anoint gently the sick and infirmed.

Today, high on top of the magnificent, illuminated dome of St. Joseph's Oratory, a lit cross shines brightly, much like the star of

Bethlehem, guiding millions of pilgrims in their desire to pay homage to our Lord and King as well as to a simple, holy man whose gifts brought hope and healing to many. We look to the Cross and we look to André to help us find our Savior, so that we, too, may bring our diverse gifts to him. In our giving, we just may find that we ourselves have received a far greater gift—that special gift of hope that only he can give.

Paul Bednarczyk, C.S.C.

CONTRIBUTORS

Agele, C.—Wed., Week 1
Ahumada, J.—Sat., Week 1
Baker, R.—Wed., Week 2
Bednarczyk, P.—Jan. 6
Britto, J.—Fri., Week 3
Burke, K.—Thurs., Week 3
Clossey, P. A.—Fri., Week 1
Cornell, P.—Jan. 1
DelFra, L.—Dec. 24
Dionne, G.—Dec. 23
Doyle, T.—Jan. 3
Dzeikan, T.—Dec. 31
Fenstermaker, J.—Dec. 27
Fortin, T.—Tues., Week 3
Gallagher, J.—Jan. 4
Giallanza, J.—Sun., Week 2
Gordon, C.—Sun., Week 4
Haders, K.—Fri., Week 2
Herman, J.—Dec. 28
Hesburgh, T.—Dec. 20
Jarret, P.—Mon., Week 1
Kayajan, D.—Thurs., Week 2
Kinberger, M. K.—Tues., Week 1
Knowles, C.—Mon., Week 2

Koeth, S.—Sun., Week 3
LeBoeuf, C.—Holy Family
McDonald, J.—Dec. 18
Monteiro, L.—Dec .26
Naudet, H.—Thurs., Week 1
Pajakowski, M. A.—Jan. 5
Papenfuss, R.—Mon., Week 3
Paquette, C.—Dec. 22
Phalan, J.—Wed., Week 3
Richard, A.—Tues., Week 2
Rozario, M.—Dec. 19
Schimmel, E.—Dec. 30
Tennyson, S.—Dec. 29
Tolentino, B.—Sat., Week 2
Vaughan, M. E.—Dec. 25
Wack, B.—Sun., Week 1
Wack, N.—Dec. 17
Wahler, M. L.—Dec. 21
Ybarra, P.—Jan. 2

ANDREW GAWRYCH, C.S.C., graduated from the University of Notre Dame with a Bachelor of Arts degree in Government and International Relations in 2002. He received a Master of Divinity degree from the University of Notre Dame in 2007 and was ordained a priest in the Congregation of Holy Cross in 2008. He currently serves at St. John Vianney Catholic Church in Phoenix, Arizona. He and Kevin Grove, C.S.C., co-edited *The Cross, Our Only Hope: Daily Reflections in the Holy Cross Tradition* (2008).

Celebrate the Holy Cross Tradition

The Gift of the Cross
Lenten Reflections in the Holy Cross Tradition
Edited by Andrew Gawrych, C.S.C.
This Lenten meditation booklet features daily reflections by priests, brothers, and sisters of the Holy Cross community.
ISBN: 9781594712029 / 96 pages / $3.50

CONGREGATION OF
HOLY CROSS
EDUCATION · PARISH · MISSION

The Cross, Our Only Hope
Daily Reflections in the Holy Cross Tradition
Edited by Andrew Gawrych, C.S.C., and Kevin Grove, C.S.C.
Foreword by Hugh Cleary, C.S.C.
Members of the Congregation of Holy Cross offer an introduction to the rich, vibrant spirituality of the Congregation in this daily meditation book.
ISBN: 9781594711626 / 512 pages / $17.95

ave maria press® • Notre Dame, Indiana • www.avemariapress.com
E-mail: avemariapress.1@nd.edu • Ph: 1-800-282-1865 • Fax: 1-800-282-5681
A Ministry of the Indiana Province of Holy Cross

Prices subject to change.

Promo Code: FH8060917B6